Puns: The Highest Form of Humor

Puns: The Highest Form of Humor

Collected and Compiled

by

James E. Taulman

Printed in the United States of America

Published by

Familystories Press
8072 Sunrise Circle
Franklin, Tennessee 37067
Familystories-4-U.com
615-595-2597

The cartoon on the cover is used with the generous permission of Colby Jones. More of his work can be seen at http://sircolby.com/cartoons/a-pastor-a-priest-and-a-rabbi/.

Dedicated to

Rob Jasper

who needled me
sew I would finish this book

Table of Contents

Puns: The Highest Form of Humor

Introduction

This is a book of groans! A punster is not looking so much for laughs as for groans when he or she delivers a pun.

One definition of a pun is "a form of joking in which a person uses a word in two senses."[1] Based on this definition, some of the material in this book technically could not be considered puns—more like plays on words or in some cases just one-line jokes. But for the most part they are close enough to puns for our broader purpose.

Most puns are not original. They have been around for years, and are told and retold, adapted and retold. For this reason, I have not even attempted to give attribution in most cases. However, one or two puns are so unique that I felt it was only proper to cite my source. But for the most part, these puns have been around and around; many of them I heard as a teenager. They appeared in one era, but they often resurface in a slightly different format in a different area. The Internet has made them accessible to us in greater numbers. They can be found on several sites and in several formats.

It has been fun to work with this material. I just wish I could remember all these puns! I could become a stand-up comic if my memory were better.

I am convinced that laughter is good medicine. Proverbs 17:22 states, "Being cheerful keeps you healthy. It is slow death to be gloomy all the time" (GNB). Or as another translation puts it, "A cheerful heart is good medicine, but a crushed spirit dries up the bones" (NIV). Any way you look at it, laughter is good for body and soul.

There are many puns available that you would not want to tell your children. But hopefully, every pun in this book would pass the "child-proof" test. Humor does not have to be filthy. As one of the puns sates, "I used to have a problem with soap, but I'm clean now." I hope all these puns are, too!

Enjoy, groan, smile, laugh—whatever response you care to make. If you have any of these reactions, then I will have accomplished my purpose.

Jim Taulman
Franklin, Tennessee
January 2017

---

1.   https://www.merriam-webster.com/dictionary/pun : accessed January 9, 2017.

1.
General

Our Boy Scout knot-tying class went off without a hitch

I've never taken an elevator to the basement floor; that's just beneath me.

I usually take steps to avoid elevators.

With hindsight, I wouldn't have sat on that thumbtack.

Two pencils decided to have a race; the outcome was a draw.

Over the years elevators have had their fair share of ups and downs in terms of popularity, but thankfully the idea has not been shafted.

Sometimes a pencil sharpener is needed to make a good point

A relief map shows where the restrooms are.

When he fell in the wet concrete, he left a bad impression.

We never really grow up; we only learn how to act in public.

War does not determine who is right; only who is left.

If towels could tell jokes, they would probably have a dry sense of humor.

In filling out an application, where it says, "In case of emergency, Notify. I put doctor.

You're never too old to learn something stupid.

I'm supposed to respect my elders, but it's getting harder and harder for me to find one now.

Exit signs; they're on the way out.

The inventor of the door knocker should win a no-bell prize

I saw a sign in a store: Puppets for free. No strings attached.

A new type of broom came out, and it's sweeping the nation.

The other day I held the door open for a clown; I thought it was a nice jester.

The dead batteries were given out free of charge.

I owe a lot to the sidewalks; they've been keeping me off the streets for years.

What do you receive when you ask a lemon for help? Lemonaid.

I feel sorry for shopping carts; they're always getting pushed around.

Whoever invented the Knock-Knock jokes should get a No-Bell Prize

What do you get if you cross a bullet and a tree with no leaves? A cartridge in a bare tree.

If something shipped by a car is called a shipment, why is something delivered by boat called a cargo?

Jim: What do you call a snobbish criminal going down the stairs? Joe: A condescending con descending.

I thought Santa was going to be late, but he arrived in the Nick of time.

A cannonball is a party for artillerymen.

My friend started telling me skeleton puns; they were all very rib tickling.

Where do you imprison a skeleton? In a rib cage.

I used to have a bad record with soap, but now my slate is clean.

When the maid found my lottery ticket she really cleaned up.

If the ocean had a personality, it would be salty.

What do you call a bald monster who lives in the lake? A lock-less monster.

Pencil sharpeners have a tough life—they live off tips.

What happened to the rich guy with the double chin? He made a four chin.

I didn't used to like duct tape at first, but then I became very attached to it.

What do you get when you cross a joke with a rhetorical question?

Television is a medium because anything well done is rare.

It is so cold outside I saw a politician with his hands in his own pockets.

I asked my North Korean friend how it was to live in North Korea. He said he can't complain.

One state official to the other: I don't know what people have against us. We haven't done anything.

A woman caught her husband on the scales sucking in his stomach. "That won't help you, Joe, you know?" "Oh it helps a lot," said Joe. "It's the only way I can see the numbers!"

Important note from a car manual: *Backing rapidly at a tree significantly reduces your trunk space.*

What kind of a driver doesn't know how to drive? A screwdriver.

I slept on a three-season bed last night; it didn't have a spring.

Puns: The Highest Form of Humor

2.

English Grammar

When asked if I were bilingual, I was about to say I knew sign language, but I figured it was sort of a mute point.

He recited verse from the bench because he was a poetic justice.

Writer's cramp is also known as Authoritis.

The English Teacher felt odd after being fired: it was post-grammatic stress disorder.

To steal ideas from one person is plagiarism; to steal from many is research.

The past present and future walked into a bar; it was tense.

A prisoner's favorite punctuation mark is the period; it marks the end of his sentence.

Double negatives are a complete NO-NO.

Proper punctuation can make the difference between a sentence that's well-written, and a sentence that's, well, written.

What is the difference between a cat and a comma? A cat has claws at the end of its paws, and a comma has a pause at the end of its clause.

Braille is easy once you get the feel of it.

I once went out with an apostrophe, but she was so possessive.

Jim: I was just thinking about you. Joe: That's an interesting letter.

At all stages Shakespeare was a playful character!

An MIT linguistics professor was lecturing his class the other day. He said, "In English a double negative forms a positive. However, in some languages, such as Russian, a double negative remains a negative. But there isn't a single language, not one, in which a double positive can express a negative". A voice from the back of the room piped up, "Yeah, right."

What's the difference between an etymologist and an entomologist? An etymologist knows the difference.

It's hard to explain puns to kleptomaniacs because they always take things literally.

Puns: The Highest Form of Humor

3.

Dentists

No one knew she had a dental implant until it came out in a conversation.
The dentist put braces on his patient as a stop-gap measure.
I got a gold filling and put my money where my mouth is.
Contemplating my imminent root canal procedure was deeply unnerving.
My cavity wasn't fixed by my regular dentist, but by a guy who was filling in.
Dentists have their own flossify on how to keep teeth clean.
They called him the king of the dentists because he specialized in crowns.
The dentist's alibi was full of holes, so the police performed a cavity search.
A lawyer asked his dentist to give him a retainer.
Dentists practice by going through many drills.
A dentist gets on everybody's nerves.
Dentists don't like a hard day at the orifice.
The dentist's favorite store at the mall is The Gap.

Dad: "Don't you feel better now, that you've gone to the dentist?" Son: "Sure do. He wasn't in."

I went to the dentist without lunch, and he gave me a plate.

I've been to the dentist several times so I know the drill.

My toothache is driving me to extraction.

"Please scream as loudly as you possibly can," said the dentist to his patient. The confused patient asked, "Why should I do that?" "The waiting room's full, and the football game starts in ten minutes."

Did you hear about the Buddhist who refused a Novocain injection during root canal treatment? He wanted to transcend dental medication.

Be nice to your dentist. They have fillings too.

What did the dentist see at the North Pole? A molar bear.

I've just seen a dentist having a big row with a manicurist. They fought tooth and nail.

What do you call a dentist who doesn't like tea? Denis.

Puns: The Highest Form of Humor

4.

Medical Doctors

A Freudian slip is when you say one thing but mean a mother.

The surgeon failed to repair his own ruptured pericardium because his heart just wasn't in it.

Don't trust people who do acupuncture; they're back stabbers.

Smaller babies may be delivered by stork, but the heavier ones need a crane.

Jill broke her finger today, but on the other hand she was completely fine.

We need a 12-step group for compulsive talkers. They could call it On Anon Anon.

Doctors tell us there are over seven million people who are overweight. These, of course, are only round figures.

The dermatologist was an avid gardener, but he had a problem with moles.

When the doctor asked the editor how he was doing, the editor said he had a problem with his circulation.

I chose my gastroenterologist based on a gut feeling.

People who nod off during long political speeches are bulldozers.

There is no point in going to an acupuncturist if you don't pin your hopes on him for full recovery.

I mixed up the cardiac resuscitation equipment with the lie detector, but I will de-fib you later.

I went to my doctor and told the receptionist that I felt like a deck of cards. She said, "Have a seat, and the doctor will deal with you when he can."

I have a bad, bad pain in my toe, no gout about it.

If you get sick at the airport it could be a terminal illness.

A hurricane is a stick used to encourage speed.

England doesn't have a kidney bank, but it does have a Liverpool

I used to be addicted to soap, but I'm clean now.

Did you hear about the guy whose whole left side was cut off? He's all right now.

Did you hear about the woman who dropped her birth control pills in the copy machine? It wouldn't reproduce for a month.

Did you hear about the guy who got hit in the head with a can of soda? He was lucky it was a soft drink.

An umbilical cord is a navel vessel.

He was hit on the head during a hailstorm and was knocked out cold.

Claustrophobic people are more productive thinking outside the box.

Did you hear about the optometrist who fell into a lens grinder and made a spectacle of himself?

A calendar went to the doctor and said, "Doc, give it to me straight? How long do I have?" The doctor replied, "You have twelve months."

"What kind of work do you do?" "Oh, I work with kidneys." "So, do you work in nephrology or in pediatric orthopedics?"

5.

Sports

The golfer was hospitalized because of too many strokes.

Two fishermen were having a discussion and opened a can of worms.

Even the best bird dog is only good to a point.

I went horseback riding the other day and broke my whip so I planted it. I'm hoping for a nice crop.

Cinderella was thrown off the basketball team because she ran away from the ball.

Horse lovers are stable people

Of all sports humor, football is my favorite. I get a kick out of the punts.

I think there are about 1 to 2 million baseball fields in the world, but that's just a ballpark number.

I'd like to buy a new boomerang please. Also, can you tell me how to throw the old one away?

One person can keep a fishing line clear, but it takes two to tangle.

You do not need a parachute to sky dive; you only need a parachute to sky dive twice.

I used to have a fear of hurdles, but I got over it.

My skiing skills are really going downhill.

My tennis opponent was not happy with my serve; he kept returning it.

I quit gymnastics because I was tired of hanging around the bars.

What do you say to impatient jockeys? Hold your horses.

A fisherman tried boxing, but he only threw hooks.

I finally found a spotter at the gym; it's like a huge weight has been lifted off my shoulders.

Why did the pig quit running the marathon? He had a problem with his hamstring.

I know you brought the wrong rock to our curling match, but we'll let it slide.

I thought dating a tennis player would be a ball, but it was just a racquet!

There was a contest on a slippery rock slope. I won in a landslide.

The long-shot was leading the Kentucky Derby, but not furlong.

The race dogs got a bad case of the fleas; they had to be scratched.

I drove around the Indianapolis Motor Speedway on my John Deere. I was on a track tour.

A novice skier often jumps to contusions.

I was overruled at the measuring competition.

The athlete claimed he long jumped over 25 feet. Actually his best jump only measured 23 feet. This was a clear case of leap fraud.

I've never killed a deer before, but I'll take a shot at it.

Attila was coaching a soccer team. He wanted them to win, but his Huns were tied.

I told the knight that I could knock him out of his saddle. Of course, I was speaking in joust.

Did you hear of the football coach who trained a chicken to fly? He ended up having a personal foul for excessive aviation.

Automatic machines that compete in sculling are rowbots.

Today a man knocked on my door and asked for a small donation towards the local swimming pool. I gave him a glass of water.

Refusing to go to the gym counts as resistance training, right?

I don't have a Fitbit, but I have a couple of fat bits.

Tell me again how I unloaded the dishwasher too loudly when you were watching golf. Detectives will want to know exactly how this went down.

6.

Animals

A zoo had a camel with no humps named Humphrey.

During branding time, cowboys have sore calves.

I have a smart pet spider; he has his own Website.

What did the buffalo say to his son when he left for college? "Bison."

Two cows were standing in a pasture when a milk truck went by proclaiming its milk was homogenized, pasteurized, Vitamin D added. One cow turned to the other and said, "Makes you feel real inefficient, doesn't it?"

Where should a dog go when it's lost its tail? The retail store of course.

I saw a sign the other day that said, "Frog parking only; all others will be toad."

One goat said to the other, "I saw a kidnapping today, but I didn't wake him up."

What's more amazing than a talking dog? A spelling bee.

My dog has no nose. How does he smell? Awful!

If it rains cats and dogs, why doesn't it reindeer?

A goose is the only thing that grows up while growing down.

Jim: If an electric eel and a sponge got married, what would their children be? Joe: Shock absorbers.

A baby seal walked into a bar. "What can I get you?" asked the bartender. "Anything but a Canadian Club," replied the seal.

What do you get from a pampered cow? Spoiled milk.

Male deer have buck teeth.

When the chimpanzee's sister had a baby, he said, "Well, I'll be a monkey's uncle."

Where did Noah keep his bees? In the ark hives.

Why do cows wear cowbells? Because their horns don't work.

Two boll weevils grew up in South Carolina. One went to Hollywood and became a famous actor. The other stayed behind in the cotton fields and never amounted to much. The second one, naturally, became known as the lesser of two weevils.

Jim: What is the purpose of reindeer? Joe: It makes the grass grow, sweetie.

What do you call a cow with no legs? Ground beef.

Jim: What would you get if you crossed a mole with a porcupine? Joe: A tunnel that leaks.

What would bears be without bees? Ears.

Two ants were eating a piece of fruit, and one of them sidled up to the other and said, "So is this a date? The other ant replied, "No, it's a fig."

Two sheep were standing in the pasture and one said to the other, "Every time I say baa, you don't have to say humbug."

Jim: What do you call a pig that does karate? Joe: Pork Chop.

Jim: What do you call a bear with no teeth? Joe: A gummy bear.

Neuter your dog—an ounce of prevention is better than a pound of cur.

Does the Little Mermaid wear an alge bra?

What do you get when you cross a snake and a plane? A Boeing Constrictor.

When milking a nervous goat, you should use kid gloves.

How can you tell if a wolf caught in a trap is from Alabama? He's chewed off three legs, and he's still in the trap.

Why did the bee get married? Because he found his honey.

What do you call a fish with no eye? FSH

Never give your uncle an anteater.

My dog used to chase people on a bike. It got so bad, I finally had to take his bike away.

What do you get when you cross-breed a cow and a shark? I don't know, but I wouldn't enjoy milking it.

What do you get if you crossbreed a sheep and a kangaroo? A woolly jumper.

Why did the calf cross the road? It wanted to get to the udder side.

Two silk worms decided to have a race; they ended in a tie.

How do you change tires on a duck? With a quackerjack, of course.

The swordfish has very few natural enemies, except the seldom seen penfish which is said to be mightier.

Why do cows have hooves instead of feet? Because they lactose.

7.

Math/Science

You know what seems odd to me? Numbers that aren't divisible by two.

Parallel lines have so much in common; it's a shame they will never meet.

To the guy who invented zero—thanks for nothing .

Never trust an atom; they make up everything.

If you do research in optics you will have to do some light reading.

Electricity doesn't know how to conduct itself.

How many sides does a circle have? Two: an inside and an outside.

Jim: Do you know what the abacus said? Joe: You can count on me.

Geometry shapes my life.

My math teacher called me average. How mean!

If I got 50 cents for every failed math exam, I'd have $6.30 now.

Why is the math book so sad? It's got too many problems,

Since light travels faster than sound, some people appear bright until you hear them speak.

Saw a street sign the other day that said, "Electric Avenue." Right below it was another sign that said, "No Outlet."

What is the difference between one yard and two yards? A fence.

You want to clone yourself? Now wouldn't that be just like you!

I saw a guy who had just touched a live electrical wire. When I asked him how he felt, he replied that it hertz a lot.

What is a nitrate? One that is much cheaper than a day rate.

Two red blood cells fell in love, but it was all in vein.

Two red blood cells were found necking in dead Earnest.

How do you measure a snake? In inches because they don't have any feet.

Support bacteria—they're the only culture some people have.

Sixteen sodiums walked into a bar followed by Batman.

There are two types of people in the world. Those who can extrapolate from incomplete data.

Know why Polish airlines only fill half of an airplane for each flight? Poles on the right half of the plane are unstable.

A photon checked into a hotel. The bellhop asked, "Can I help you with your luggage?" The photon replied, "I don't have any. I'm traveling light."

Dear Algebra, stop asking us to find your X. She is never coming back, and don't ask Y.

8.

Flying/Aviation

A man sued an airline company after it lost his luggage. Sadly, he lost his case.
To be a successful frequent flier you need a lot of connections.
When asked by a passenger how high he would get, the pilot replied, "I don't do drugs."
The airlines have become so cash-strapped that they charged me for my emotional baggage.
During his air test a young pilot flew through a rainbow. He passed with flying colors.
Traveling on a flying carpet is a rugged experience.
Did you hear about the pilot who always had work? He was great at landing a job.
The debate about unmanned aircraft strikes just keeps droning on.
The plane flight brought my acrophobia to new heights.
The cost of the space program is astronomical.

An astronaut broke the law of gravity and got a suspended sentence.

One of the first things you'll notice at the Beijing airport is a whole lot of Chinese checkers.

Some planes are so cramped that passengers suffer jet leg.

The first time I got hold of a hang glider, I had to wing it.

A spacecraft took pictures of Mars and Saturn and got the best of both worlds.

He became a sky diver out of the blue.

After a few beers on the plane, Charlie was flying high into the wild brew yonder.

Does a no-fly zone prohibit zippers?

How do you get off a non-stop flight?

Did you hear that this week NASA launched a space craft with three heifers and a bull on board thus making it the first herd shot round the world.

Puns: The Highest Form of Humor

9.

Bar Puns

Four fonts walked into a bar. The barman said, "Get out! We don't want your type in here."

A bacon sandwich walked into a bar and ordered a whiskey. "Sorry," growled the bartender, "we don't serve food here."

A group of termites marched into a saloon and asked, "Is the bar tender here?"

I was sitting in a bar one day and two really large women came in, talking in an interesting accent. So I said, "Cool accent, are you two ladies from Ireland?" One of them snarled at me, "It's Wales, dumbo!" So I corrected myself, "Oh, right, so are you two whales from Ireland?" That's about the last thing I remember.

A pastor, a priest, and a rabbi walked into a bar. The bartender looked up and said, "Is this some kind of joke?"

A skeleton walked into a bar and said, "Gimme a beer, and a mop."

A screwdriver walked into a bar, and the bartender said, "Hey, we have a drink named after you!" The screwdriver responded, "You have a drink named Murray?"

A guy walked into a bar and asked the bartender, "Do you have any helicopter flavored potato chips?" The bartender shook his head and said, "No, we only have plane."

A horse walked into a bar, and the bartender said, "So. Why the long face?"

A woman and a duck walked into a bar. The bartender said, "Where'd you get the pig." The woman said, "That's not a pig, that's a duck." He said, "I was talking to the duck."

A skunk walked into a bar and said, "Hey where did everybody go?"

E-flat walked into a bar. The bartender said, "Sorry, we don't serve minors."

A potato walked into a bar and all eyes were on him!

What do you call a Bohemian who gets thrown out of a bar? A bounced Czech.

So a guy walked into a bar after a round of golf and sat down at a table opposite a flashily dressed blonde who said to him, "I'm a hooker." He replied, "Well, if you turn your hands on the shaft a little bit to the left, you'll tend more towards a slice."

It's the Christmas season and a guy walked into a bar in Atlanta, Georgia, and noticed a Nativity Scene behind the bar. the Three Wise Men are all wearing fireman's hats. He asked the bartender why the Magi were wearing fireman's hats and the barkeep said, "Well, everyone knows that they came from afar."

So Jesus walked into a bar and said, "I'll just have a glass of water."

A guy with dyslexia walked into a bra.

A jumper cable walked into a bar. The barman said, "I'll serve you, but don't start anything."

A man walked into a bar with a slab of asphalt under his arm and said "A beer please, and one for the road."

A drunk walked into a bar. "Ouch!" he said.

10.

Food

A baker stopped making donuts after he got tired of the hole thing.

A baker always put too much flour in his bread because he was a gluten for punishment.

He told me he lost my sieve at his mother's house, but his story didn't hold water.

Knowledge is knowing a tomato is a fruit; wisdom is not putting it in a fruit salad.

What did the gingerbread man put on his bed? A cookie sheet.

"Waiter! This coffee tastes like mud.""Yes sir, it's fresh ground."

A boiled egg in the morning is hard to beat.

What do you call a cow that gives no milk? A milk dud (Joe: or an udder failure).

I bought some of that new gourmet mustard named Dijon vu. I really was disappointed; it was the same old mustard.

Did you hear that Frosty the Snowman was kicked out of the produce section at Publix? He was caught picking his nose.

I love donuts; they're not self-centered at all.

There is an email going around composed of processed pork, gelatin, and salt in a can. If you get this email, do not open it; it's Spam.

Jim: What kind of peppers wear scarves? Joe: Chilly peppers.

I'd tell you a joke about a cow, but I always butcher it.

I was scrambling for another egg joke, but I can't seem to whip one up. Guess I'm a bit fried.

Did you hear about the lost sausage? It was the missing link.

The defendant in a coffee theft trial refused to testify on the grounds that could incriminate him.

I told Riley she eats too many pickles. She said to dill with it.

I've been eating a lot of pasta lately; I think it's becoming a part of my daily rotini!

Those who enjoy life while eating hot dogs are relishing the moment.

What kind of pumpkin protects castles? A royal gourd!

When I told them about how I escaped my pumpkin prison, they said I was out of my gourd.

Drinking too much coffee can cause a latte problems.

Stealing someone's coffee is called "mugging."

Coffee has bean the grounds of many a heated and strong discussion.

When he spilled coffee on her shirt, she showed him dis-stain.

A butcher was trying so hard to be funny, but he just wasn't making the cut.

I wanted to grow my own food, but I couldn't get bacon seeds anywhere.

Q. Why do the French like to eat snails so much? A. They can't stand fast food.

I had to decide between making salad with my mom or playing catch with my dad. It was a toss-up.

Two peanuts were walking in a tough neighborhood, and one of them was a-salted.

A farmer raises wheat in dry weather; in wet weather he raises an umbrella.

I went to Red Lobster for their endless shrimp, and my wife accused me of being shellfish.

I ordered a chicken and an egg off the Internet; I wanted to see which came first.

It was a terrible summer for Humpty Dumpty, but he had a great fall.

The crusty, ill-tempered baker was a scone's throw from becoming toast.

I eat my tacos over a tortilla. That way when stuff falls out, BOOM, another taco.

One day you're the best thing since sliced bread; the next, you're toast.

Turning vegan is a big missed steak.

How come "You're a peach" is a complement, but "You're bananas" is an insult? Why are we allowing fruit discrimination to tear society apart?

Every time someone calls me fat I get so depress I cut myself . . . another piece of cake.

An instructor at an ice cream parlor is a sundae school teacher

11. Occupations

He used to repair televisions, but his business went down the tubes.
She didn't like her masseuse; she rubbed her the wrong way.
If you operate a drill press, you have a boring job.
My job at the concrete plant seems to get harder and harder.
Since Bruce got too close to the big blade at the saw mill, he is no longer feeling chipper.
Charles fell into the meat grinder; now he's ground Chuck.
The novice executioner couldn't get the hang of it.
Real estate agents believe in doing good deeds.
Retired teachers are classless.
Do shepherds sometimes have staff meetings?

For a while, Houdini used a lot of trap doors in his act, but he was just going through a stage.

He wanted to build a rope factory, but first he had to pull a few strings.

Never lie to x-ray technicians; they can see right through you.

A bacteria walked into a bar and the bartender said, "We don't serve bacteria in this place." The bacteria said, "But I work here; I'm staph."

A janitor with a broom in hand swept her off her feet.

He only knew how to drive a forklift in reverse; he was the backup man.

We'll never run out of math teachers because they always multiply.

The farmer gave his chickens a bushel of feed, but they only took a peck.

The girl quit her job at the dough nut factory because she was fed up with the hole business.

The experienced carpenter really nailed it, but the new guy screwed everything up.

John Deere's manure spreader is the only piece of equipment the company won't stand behind.

Regular visitors to the dentist are familiar with the drill.

My first job was working in an orange juice factory, but I got canned because I couldn't concentrate.

She was only a whiskey maker, but he loved her still.

I used to be a blackjack host, but I was offered a better deal.

I used to work in a blanket factory, but it folded.

I wanted to be a butcher, but I didn't make the cut.

The linen shop gave their employees free bedding. Even their accountant had her own handmade spread sheet.

The hotel chef was noted for his tomfoolery and his capers.

When the thimble factory went on a strike, many people got stuck without one.

Did you hear about the farmer who got attacked by a cow? He milked it for all it was worth.

I got a job in the transmission shop. It's shift work.

I saw this guy walking into court carrying a large box. Ten minutes later he came out; it was a briefcase.

Tree trimmers do such a fantastic job, they should take a bough.

He knew his lot in life was to create the world's greatest mosquito repellent; he had a deet with destiny.

The new president of the local Climate Changes Committee was the carbon copy of his predecessor.

My friend quit working at the pin factory; he felt there was no point to the job.

I used to do balance and rotations at an auto shop, but I felt like I was just spinning my wheels and decided to retire.

How do construction workers party? They raise the roof.

After manually rotating the heavy machinery, the worker grew very cranky.

The stripper was getting tired of the same old thong and dance.

"I am presently employed," said the gift wrapper.

The inept psychic attempted clairvoyance but just couldn't get intuit.

Puns: The Highest Form of Humor

The chimney sweep wore a soot and tie.

Fishermen are reel men.

The carpenter came around the other day; he made the best entrance I have ever seen.

What happens when a cop gets into bed? He becomes an undercover cop.

Installing a new bathroom fan is exhausting.

A professor without a pointer may find that his lecture is pointless.

One evening King Arthur's men discovered Sir Lancelot's moonshine whiskey operation and shattered the still of the knight.

Did you hear about the magician who walked down the street and turned into a drugstore?

Puns: The Highest Form of Humor

12.

Dating and Marriage

I knew a woman who owned a taser; man was she stunning!

It was an emotional wedding; even the cake was in tiers.

She didn't marry the gardener; he was too rough around the hedges.

She stole the policeman's heart, but he made a cardiac arrest.

I had a date with a girl who had a wooden leg, but I broke it.

The last thing I want to do is hurt you, but it's still on my list.

A male snake charmer married a female undertaker. Their bath towels read *Hiss*, and *Hearse*.

A shotgun wedding is a case of wife or death.

In high school my old girl friend stopped me as I was walking down the hall with my new girlfriend and said, "You may have chemistry with her, but you have history with me."

If a girl from Iceland and a guy from Cuba have a kid, will he be an Icecube?

Some couples don't go to the gym because some relationships don't work out.

I'm no photographer, but I can picture us together.

A wife complained to her husband, "Just look at that couple down the road; how lovely they are. He keeps holding her hand, kissing her, holding the door for her. Why can't you do the same?" "Are you mad? I barely know the woman!"

My ex-wife still misses me, but her aim is steadily improving.

One palm tree said to another, "Let's have a date."

The two desk lamps were considered to be social lights because they kept going out at night together.

Q: Why did the lights go out? A: They liked each other a lot.

My wife is always cold so I told her to stand in the corner; corners are always 90 degrees.

My wife told me to stop impersonating a flamingo; I had to put my foot down.

Confucius says Love one another. If it doesn't work, just interchange the last two words.

Why is the man who invests all your money called a broker?

13.

Music

He tried to play the shoehorn but got only footnotes.

What do you get when you drop a piano down a mineshaft? A flat miner

A musician tripped over a chord, which resulted in a nasty note.

Vinyl records are really groovy.

The two pianists had a good marriage; they always were in a chord.

"What's the difference between a piano, a tuna fish, and a tub of glue?" "You can tune a piano, but you can't piano a tuna." "What about the tub of glue?" "I knew you'd get stuck on that."

I heard about a new band called Ceiling, and all their fans were called ceiling fans.

After three days of fishing, the musician still had not caught a bassoon.

Goats in France are musical because they have French horns.

What rock group has four men that don't sing? Mount Rushmore.

Mmm! These cello pudding pops are amazing!

We've really got to guitar act together.

"Why did you banjo?" "She was just too vocal."

She's a great girl—you should meter next time!

This ring cymbalizes so much to me.

I didn't mean to harp on you about it.

Are you calling me a lyre?

Puns: The Highest Form of Humor

14.

Religion

There's a sin dividing line between heaven and hell.
Atheists don't solve exponential equations because they don't believe in higher powers.
When cannibals ate a missionary, they got a taste of religion.
There is no conclusive evidence about what happens to old skeptics, but their future is doubtful.
I considered going into the ministry, but I didn't have an altar ego.
Do you know how the sky was created? It was airborne.

If you fill an hour glass with quick sand, will it run through faster?

Crucifixion is done after cross examination!

A contest between church choirs is the battle of the choral see.

Why can't you trust Satan's resume? The devil lies in the details.

So what if I don't know what apocalypse means? It's not the end of the world!

I was going to tell you a joke about infinity, but it didn't have an ending!

Atheism is a non-prophet organization.

Cannibals don't eat divorced people because they're bitter.

God gave us the brain to work out problems. However, we use it to create more problems.

If you're going through hell, keep going.

https://www.pinterest.com/pin/278449189438733059/ : accessed January 5, 2017.

Puns: The Highest Form of Humor

15.

Computers and Business

If Apple made a car, would it have Windows?

I changed my iPhone's name to Titanic. It's syncing now.

Jim: Our grandson has his grandmother on speed dial. Joe: I guess that is instagram.

I love Wi-Fi so much because we just have that connection.

I used to sell computer parts, but then I lost my drive.

Forrest Gump's password is *1Forrest1*.

Following last week's news that the Origami Bank had folded, we are hearing that Sumo Bank has gone belly up and the Bonsai Bank plans to cut back some of its branches. Karaoke Bank is up for sale and is going for a song.

Cash cows control bull market stocks!

Two cell phones met, and one said, "Why are you wearing glasses?" The other replied, "I lost all my contacts."

When my boss asked me who is the stupid one, me or him? I told him everyone knew he didn't hire stupid people.

Behind every successful student, there is a deactivated Facebook account.

Sign on the door of an internet hacker, "Gone Phishing.'"

A computer technician received third degree burns when he touched the firewall.

Backups are usually a good thing unless it's a sewer.

A new computer shop has just opened up. It is located on Boot Drive.

After punching his computer and breaking his hand, the guy required tech knuckle support.

The lumberjack loved his new computer. He especially enjoyed logging in.

I should have been sad when my flashlight batteries died, but I was delighted.

I shouldn't have plugged my iPhone into the PC at the kitchen. It's now in the sync.

Talking to her about computer hardware, I make my mother board.

I dropped a computer on my toes and had megahertz.

When the spammer's computer exploded, it blew him to kingdom.com.

Will this computer last five years? Obsoletely!

I got a deal on a new computer, and they threw in the operating system to boot.

I crossed a cell phone with a skunk, and now the service stinks.

They came out with a GPS device for bird watchers that has tern by tern directions.

I tried to update my computer this morning, but it wouldn't work. After several attempts, I had that syncing feeling.

I bought a computer from The Nero Company. It comes with a CD/Rome burner.

Did you hear about the man who got his finger stuck in his computer? He was trying to insert his thumb drive.

Buying a cheap mouse could leave you with a squeak and a sad tale.

People who plug their computer keyboards into hi-fi systems aren't idiots; they are stereotyping.

Two ships were traveling from China to the U. S. One was loaded with blue paint, and the other carried red paint. In the middle of a storm, the two ships collided; they were all marooned.

16.

Family

The little old woman who lived in a shoe wasn't the sole owner; there were strings attached.

In the room the curtains were drawn, but the rest of the furniture was real.

A family named Woods has a large family tree. You often can't see the tree for the Woods.

I bought my wife a bag and a belt for her birthday. We'll have that vacuum cleaner working in no time.

Children who fail their coloring exams always need a shoulder to crayon.

The Balloon family name died off when it ran out of heir.

My first child has gone off to college, and I feel a great emptiness in my life—specifically, in my checking account.

I think Santa has riverfront property in Brazil. All our presents came from Amazon this year.

Arranging Goliath's funeral was a giant undertaking.

My daughter asked me if I was having fun doing the laundry. I replied, "Loads.'"

This year I made my Christmas wreath out of Franklin Fir branches. I really like a wreath of Franklin.

I heard Einstein got along well with his parents—relatively speaking.

I really regretted the inconsiderate comment I made. It was rued.

What did the mama tire and the papa tire name their baby girl tire? Michelle Lynn.

My neighbor's sprinkler is a constant irrigation to me.

My cousin has a callus on only one foot. Does that make her a unicorn?

I knew my wife was pregnant when she looked at me with fertilize.

Some doting parents are son worshipers.

The mother kangaroo tried to instill good financial habits in her baby. She told him to pocket all his allowance.

Did you hear about the builder, who was retiring, and said to his son, "This is all yours now, Son." His son said thoughtfully, "I dunno, Dad. You're a hard hat to follow!"

My grandma always gives me the benefit of the dote.

Why did the cannibal eat his wife and children? He was familyished!

Two cannibals were sitting by a fire. The first said, "Gee, I hate my mother-in-law." The second replied, "So, try the potatoes."

Puns: The Highest Form of Humor

17.

Clothes and Dress

What is the difference between a nicely dressed man on a tricycle and a poorly dressed man on a bicycle? A tire.

What did the hat say to the tie? "You hang around, and I'll go on a head."

What are half-sized quartz watches? Pintz watches.

The man's zipper on his pants broke, but he fixed it on the fly.

I really wanted a camouflage shirt, but I couldn't find one.

I tried wearing tight jeans, but I could never pull it off.

I planned to find my watch today, but I didn't have the time.

I tinted my hair today; it was the highlight of my day.

Learning to walk in high heels will keep you on your toes.

Thieves broke into my house and stole everything except my soap, shower gel, towels, and deodorant. Dirty scoundrels.

Did you hear about these new reversible jackets? I'm excited to see how they turn out.

Jim: I keep noticing this guy at church whose pants are always wrinkled. Joe: I bet he has an iron deficiency.

Did you hear about the man in boxers that the police arrested? He led them on a brief chase.

Have you got bills to pay? If you do, please give it back; he looks silly bald.

Now that they allow us to wear jeans at the office everyday, I am no longer a slacker.

If you wear cowboy clothes, are you ranch dressing?

I heard a bunch of sewing jokes the other day. They were strung seamlessly together.

What is the difference between a well-dressed man and a dog? The man wears a suit, the dog just pants.

Puns: The Highest Form of Humor

18.

Attitudes and Behaviors

Losing your head in an emergency is a no brainer.

I was going to buy a book on phobias, but I was afraid it wouldn't help me.

If I agreed with you, we'd both be wrong.

I didn't say it was your fault; I said I was blaming you.

I used to be indecisive; now I'm not so sure.

Someone once told me to follow my dreams, so I'm going back to bed.

People who choose cremation over traditional burial are thinking outside the box.

The only time you should not give 100 percent is when you are giving blood.

Show me someone in denial, and I'll show you a person in Egypt up to his ankles in water.

Jim: Why do people who throw away feather pillows get depressed? Joe: Their down is in the dumps.

Weight loss pills stolen this morning; police say suspects are still at large.

Are you a sleepy skeleton? You look bone tired.

Are people who are afraid of Santa Claus claustrophobic?

I saw an ad for burial plots and thought to myself: *This is the last thing I need.*

My IQ test results just came in, and I'm quite relieved. Thank God it's negative.

The nice thing about egotists is that they don't talk about other people.

I am so poor I can't even pay attention.

An optimist sees light at the end of a tunnel and thinks it's an exit. A pessimist sees light at the end of a tunnel and assumes it is an onrushing train. The train conductor sees two stupid guys staggering on train tracks.

Will glass coffins be a success? Remains to be seen.

I saw a sign at a yard sale that read: *Radio for sale. Volume stuck on full.* I said, "I can't turn that down."

Jim: My sister treats me like Lucy treats Linus. Joe: Sounds like you've got analogy to Peanuts.

Saw a sign the other day that said The Hokey Pokey Clinic. I guess that would be a place to turn yourself around.

I can totally keep secrets; it's the people I tell them to who can't.

My therapist says I have a preoccupation with vengeance. We'll see about that.

You're not fat, you're just—easier to see.

If you can smile when things go wrong, you have someone in mind to blame.

The 50-50-90 rule: Anytime you have a 50–50 chance of getting something right, there's a 90 percent probability you'll get it wrong.

Team work is important; it helps to put the blame on someone else.

I've been repeating the same mistakes in life for so long now, I think I'll start calling them traditions.

Before I criticize a man, I like to walk a mile in his shoes. That way, when I do criticize him, I'm a mile away, and I have his shoes.

Women spend more time wondering what men are thinking than men spend time thinking.

Funny how when someone says we need to talk, they really mean you need to listen to what she has to say.

I am a nobody; nobody is perfect; therefore I am perfect.

I entered what I ate today into my new fitness app, and it just sent an ambulance to my house.

I sometimes watch birds and wonder If I could fly who would I drop on?"

Nothing ruins a Friday more than an understanding that today is just Thursday.

She wanted a puppy, but I didn't want a puppy. So we compromised and got a puppy.

You're the reason the gene pool needs a lifeguard.

My kids are very optimistic. Every glass they leave sitting around the house is at least half full.

I am known at the gym as the before picture.

A positive attitude may not solve all your problems, but it will annoy enough people to make it worth the effort.

I've put something aside for a rainy day; it's called an umbrella.

It must be difficult to post inspirational Tweets when your blood type is B Negative

I get plenty of exercise—jumping to conclusions, pushing my luck, and dodging deadlines.

Whenever I find the key to success, someone changes the lock.

I was going to quit all my bad habits for the new year, but then I remembered that nobody likes a quitter.

Where there's a will, I want to be in it.

19.
Cops and Robbers

Two inmates broke out of an Oklahoma City jail by climbing through a vent in the shower room. They made a clean get away.

The man entered his home and was absolutely delighted to find that someone had stolen all his lamps.

Some undercover operatives are given blanket approvals.

Obituaries of those hanged in the old west used to be posted in the noose paper.

When the gunman walked in, he turned the store into a flee market.

I was accused of stealing a house, but all charges were dropped as the claims were without foundation.

Late one night a mugger wearing a mask stopped a well-dressed man and stuck a gun in his ribs. "Give me your money," he demanded. Scandalized, the man replied, "You can't do this—I'm a U.S. Congressman!" "Oh! In that case," smiled the robber, "Give me MY money!"

What do you get when you pour cement on a burglar? A hardened criminal.

When the shocked IRS agent was found guilty of tax evasion, he had to take time to collect himself.

What do you call a clairvoyant midget who escaped from prison? A small medium at large.

A police recruit was asked during the exam, "What would you do if you had to arrest your own mother?" He replied, "Call for backup."

How do police officers hand cuff a one armed man?

When stopped by the police be certain the birthday you give matches the age you gave when lying about your birthday.

A criminal's best asset is his lie ability.

The two guys caught drinking battery acid will soon be charged.

Why was the ink drop sad? Because her dad was in the pen, and she didn't know how long the sentence would be!

Prison walls are never built to scale.

A nut named Hazel held up a bank saying, "Give me all the cashew have."

The warden gave the inmates acne medicine hoping it would keep them from breaking out.

Employed by his jailbird father-in-law, a guy soon realized that when an in-law works for an outlaw, income depends on outcome.

He threw jello at his wife, who had him arrested for carrying a congealed weapon.

A lingerie thief gave a police officer the slip.

Stolen eggs are poached.

A librarian caught stealing had the book thrown at her and was put in a three storey jail.

Who do you call when Zika infected mosquitoes attack? The SWAT team.

Puns: The Highest Form of Humor

20.

International Puns

Those who jump off a Paris bridge are in Seine.

A grenade thrown into a kitchen in France would result in Linoleum Blownapart.

Visitors to Cuba are usually Havana good time.

Never make fun of a Scotsman's traditional garb; you could get kilt that way.

The Irish should be rich because their capital is always Dublin.

The incontinent Scotsman had a wee accident.

I used to like Russian dolls until I realized they were full of themselves.

The pharaohs of Egypt worked out the first pyramid scheme.

If you send a letter to the Philippines, do you have to use a Manila envelope?

It's a lengthy article on Japanese sword fighters, but I can Samurais it for you.

It is tough to do inventories in Afghanistan because of the tally ban.

What nationality is Santa Claus? North Polish.

Sir Lancelot once had a very bad dream about his horse. It was a knight mare.

Saw a lady at the grocery store who had a banner across her chest that read, "Miss France." When I asked her if she was in a beauty pageant, she replied, "No, I just miss France."

What do you call a secondhand clothing store in India? Whose Sari Now.

A Greek playwright entered a tailor shop and handed the tailor a pair of torn pants. The tailor looked up at him and asked, "Euripides?" The tragedian responded, "Yes, Eumenides?"

Does the name Pavlov ring a bell?

In a democracy it's your vote that counts; in feudalism, it's your count that votes.

Local Area Network in Australia: the LAN down under.

I thought I saw an eye doctor on an Alaskan island, but it turned out to be an optical Aleutian.

Italian building inspectors in Pisa are leanient.

Before the revolution, Russia was in a Tsary state.

When Irish boys carry their little brothers, they get a Pat on the back.

"Should we watch the Swiss?" "Of quartz we should."

Puns: The Highest Form of Humor

21.

List Of Punny Book Titles

Bee Stings Are in the Hand of the Bee Holder, By A. P. Airy
Dull Pain, By A. King
Electrical Wiring Made Easy, By A. C. Deesey
I Like Fish, By Ann Chovie
In Year One, By A. D. Calendar
Let's Play Billiards, By A. Q. Ball
Morning Radio, By A. M. Effem
Mountain Climbing, By Andover Hand
Not a Guitar! Amanda Lynne
Not Very Expensive, By Amir Pittance
Ouch! By A. B. Stung
Robotics Handbook, By A. I. Expert
Roger Wilco, By A. O. Kaye
Singing Without an Orchestra, By A. K. Pella
The Irish Heart Surgeon, By Angie O'Plasty
The Old Codger, By A. T. Yearsold
The Unknown Rodent, By A. Nonny Mouse

Theft and Robbery, By Andy Tover
This Is Not Optional, By Amanda Tory
Unemployed, By Anita Job
Uninteresting Road Signs, By Bill Bored
Unknown Rodent, By A. Nonny Mouse
Unsolved Murders, By Mr. E
Unsolved Mysteries, By N. Igma
Upstream, By Sam N. Fishing
Urban Areas, By Bill Tupp
Vacation in France, By Hugo Down
Vacationing in Europe, By A. Broad
Vegas, By Candyce Rolle
Vegetable Arrangements, By Arty Choke
Vegetarian Cooking, By Jeffrey Dahlmer
Very Precise, By Matt Iculous
Volunteer's Guidebook, By Linda Hand
Vowel Promissory Notes, By A. E. I. O'You

Wake Up! By Sal Ammoniac

War Injuries I Have Seen, By V. A. Hospital

Waste Water, By Sue Ridgepipe

Waterways of the World, By Sue S. Canal

We All Need This! By S. N. Shall

We Solve Mysteries, By P. I. Detective

We Take Credit Cards, But . . . , By Cassius Better

We Won 20–1! By Barry Um

We're All Flakes, By Dan Druff

Webster's Words, By Dick Shunnary

Weekend in Hong Kong, By Rick Shaw

Weepy Movie, By Maud Lynn Story

Well, I Never! By I. D. Claire

West Coast Universities, By Stan Ford

What Anne Did with Her Pencils, By Andrew Pictures

What I Dance To, By D. J. Music

What I Really Want, By Trudie Zire

What Makes Airplanes Go, By Jeff Fuel

What Makes Army People Sick, By P. X. Food

What Music Used to Be On, By L. P. Record

What to Do if You're in a Car Accident, By Rhea Ender

What to Do with Your Invention, By Pat Tent

What's for Breakfast? By Hammond Eggs

What's for Dinner? By Chuck Roast

What's Green, Yet Does Not Grow? By U. S. Dollar

What's Up Doc? By Howie Dewin

What's Your Invention? By Pat Tent

Whatchamacallit!, By Thingum Bob

When Baseball Heroes Strike Out, By K. C. Atbatt

When's the Revolution? By Millie Tant

Where She Sells Sea Shells, By S. C. Shore

Where The World Is Going, By Helena Handbasket

Where There Are Hangings Every Day, By R. T. Museum

Where to Find Islands, By Archie Pelago

Where to Get A Road Hog, By R. V. Dealer

Where to Put Your Money, By Bill Fold

Where's My Hat? By Sonia Head

Who Cares? By A. Y. Nott

Who Killed Cock Robin? By B. B. Gunn

Who Killed Cock Robin? By Howard I. Know

Whose Face Can Launch 1,000 Ships? By L. N. Otroy

Why Cars Stop, By M. T. Tank

Why Do People Avoid Me? By B. O. Problem

Why Our Dumps Are Filling Up, By X. S. Waste

Why Software Is Buggy, By Q. A. Tester

Why There Are No Jokes on Humor, By I. M. Just & Jo King

Why Women Exercise, By Hy Bunz

Will He or Won't He? By Mae B. Sew

Will You Marry Me? By S. I. Will

Wind in the Maple Trees, By Russell Ingleaves

Wind Instruments, By Tom Bone

Winning at Golf, By T. Off

Winning the Race, By Vic Tree

Wish I'd Never Been Born, By Rudy Daye

Within the Law, By Lee Gull

Without Warning, By Oliver Sudden

Working in a Nursing Home, By K. R. Giver

Worms, By Earl E. Byrd

Woulda Been a Great Shortstop, By Kent Hitt

Wouldn't You Know It, By Murphy Slaw

Yoko's Robe, By Kim Ono

You Always Get Caught, By Sue Nora Later

You Drip! By Lee K. Fawcette

You Tell Me the Answer! By S. Q. Question

You Too Can Gain Weight, by Marietta Pi

You Wash, I'll Dry, By Terry Cloth

You're a Bundle of Laughs, By Vera Funny

You're Being Audited! By O. Y. Mee

You're Kidding! By Shirley U. Jest

You're So Sweet, By Mable Syrup

You're Welcome, By N. Q. Verymuch

Your Guess Is as Good as Mine, By S. T. Mate

Yours Forever, By Tillie N. Deteim

Zaftig Ladies, By C Irving Hipps"

22.

PUN JOKES

The Hungry Lion
A hungry lion was roaming through the jungle looking for something to eat. He came across two men. One was sitting under a tree and reading a book; the other was typing away on his typewriter. The lion quickly pounced on the man reading the book and devoured him. Even the king of the jungle knows that readers digest and writers cramp.

Chess at the Hotel
A group of chess enthusiasts checked into a hotel and were standing in the lobby discussing their recent tournament victories. After an hour, the manager came out of the office and asked them to disperse.
"But why?" they asked, as they moved off. "Because," he said, "I can't stand chess nuts boasting in an open foyer."

Dog in a Bar
A three-legged dog walked into a saloon in the Old West. He slid up to the bar and announced, "I'm looking for the man who shot my paw."

The Adopted Twins
A woman had twins and gave them up for adoption. One of them went to a family in Egypt and was named

Amahl. The other went to a family in Spain. They named him Juan. Years later, Juan sent a picture of himself to his birth mother. Upon receiving the picture, she told her husband that she wished she also had a picture of Amahl. He responded, "They're twins! If you've seen Juan, you've seen Amahl."

The Friar Florists

The friars were behind on their belfry payments, so they opened up a small florist shop to raise funds. Since everyone liked to buy flowers from the men of God, a rival florist across town thought this was unfair. He asked the good fathers to close down, but they would not. He went back and begged the friars to close. They ignored him. So the rival florist hired Hugh MacTaggart, the roughest and most vicious thug in town to persuade, them to close. Hugh beat up the friars and trashed their store, saying he'd be back if they didn't close up shop. Terrified, they did, thereby proving that Hugh, and only Hugh, can prevent florist friars.

The Doctor's Drink

A doctor made it his regular habit to stop off at a bar for a hazelnut daiquiri on his way home. The bartender knew his routine, and would always have the drink waiting at precisely 5:03 p.m. One afternoon, as the end of the work day approached, the bartender was dismayed to find he was out of hazelnut extract. Thinking quickly, he threw together a daiquiri made with hickory nuts and set it on the bar. The doctor came in at his regular time, took one sip of the drink and exclaimed, "This isn't a hazelnut daiquiri." "Yes, You're right," replied the bartender, "it's a hickory daiquiri, Doc."

Worried About Recurring Dreams

A guy went to a psychiatrist. "Doc, I keep having these alternating recurring dreams. First I'm a tepee, then I'm a wigwam, then I'm a tepee, then I'm a wigwam. It's driving me crazy. What's wrong with me?" The doctor replied, "It's very simple. You're two tents."

Surprise Breakfast

A guy went into a restaurant for a Christmas breakfast while in his home town for the holidays. After looking over the menu he said, "I'll have the eggs Benedict." When his order came it was ornately served on a big shiny chrome hubcap. "What's with the hubcap?" he asked the waiter. The waiter sang, "There's no plate like chrome for the hollandaise."

Atom Collision

Two atoms were walking down the street and they ran into each other.
One says to the other, "Are you all right?"
"No, I lost an electron." "Are you sure?" "Yeah, I'm positive."

One Happy Chief

An Indian chief had three wives, each of whom was pregnant. The first gave birth to a boy. The chief was so elated he built her a tepee made of deer hide.

A few days later, the second gave birth, also to a boy. The chief was very happy. He built her a tepee made of antelope hide. The third wife gave birth a few days later, but the chief kept the details a secret. He built this one a two story tepee, made out of a hippopotamus hide. The chief then challenged the tribe to guess what had occurred. Many tried, unsuccessfully. Finally, one young brave declared that the third wife had given birth to twin boys. "Correct," said the chief. "How did you figure it out?" The warrior answered, "It's elementary. The value of the squaw of the hippopotamus is equal to the sons of the squaws of the other two hides."

News Item

PRILEP, Yugoslavia (AP) Outside a small Macedonian village close to the border between Greece and strife-torn Yugoslavia, a lone Catholic nun keeps a quiet watch over a silent convent. She is the last caretaker of the site of significant historical developments spanning more than 2,000 years.

When Sister Maria Cyrilla of the Order of the Perpetual Watch dies, the convent of St. Elias will be closed by the Eastern Orthodox Patriarch of Macedonia. However, that isn't likely to happen soon as Sister Maria, 53, enjoys excellent health. By her own estimate, she walks ten miles daily about the grounds of the convent, which once served as a base for the army of Attila the Hun.

In more ancient times, a Greek temple to Eros, the god of love, occupied the hilltop site. Historians say that Attila took over the old temple in 439 A.D. and used it as a base for his marauding army.

The Huns are believed to have first amassed and then destroyed a large collection of Greek legal writs at the site. It is believed that Attila wanted to study the Greek legal system and had the writs and other documents brought to the temple. Scholars differ as to why he had the valuable documents destroyed—either because he was barely literate and couldn't read them, or because they provided evidence of democratic government that did not square with his own notion of rule by an all-powerful tyrant.

When the Greek church took over the site in the fifteenth century and the convent was built, church leaders ordered the pagan statue of Eros destroyed, so another ancient Greek treasure was lost.

Today, there is only the lone sister, watching over the old Hun base, amidst the strife of war-torn Yugoslavia, and when she goes, that will be it. Thus, that's how it ends, with no Huns, no writs, no Eros, and nun left on base.[1]

The Calculating Sheepdog

After a talking sheepdog got all the sheep in the pen, he reported back to the farmer. "All forty accounted for." "But I only have thirty-six sheep," said the farmer. "I know," said the sheepdog, "but I rounded them up."

1.　　See http://whosoever.org/v8i2/nun.shtml : accessed January 9, 2017. The Web site says copyrighted by the author, but I could not find the author.

Fire in a Kayak

Two Eskimos sitting in a kayak were chilly, but when they lit a fire in the craft it sank. This proves once and for all that you can't have your kayak and heat it, too.

Watch Those Indefinite Pronouns

The village blacksmith hired an enthusiastic new apprentice, willing to work long, hard hours. He instructed the boy, "When I take the shoe out of the fire, I'll lay it on the anvil. When I nod my head, you hit it with the hammer." The apprentice did exactly as he was told, and now he's the new village blacksmith.

Barbershop Blunders

The barbershop was crowded so the woman at the cash register, offered to put my name on the waiting list. "What is it?" she asked. "Stephen, with a P-H," I said. Minutes later, a chair opened up, and my name was called: "Pheven?"

What An Ugly Duck...

My husband was water skiing when he fell into the river. As the boat circled to pick him up, he noticed a hunter sitting in a duck boat in the reeds. My husband put his hands in the air and joked, "Don't shoot!" The hunter responded, "Don't quack."

Watch What You Eat

My wife, a phlebotomist at the Denver Veterans Administration Hospital, entered a patient's room to draw blood. Noticing an apple on his nightstand, she remarked, "An apple a day keeps the doctor away, right?" "That's true," the patient agreed. "I haven't seen a doctor in three days."

The Elephant and the Turtle

An elephant walked up to a river and saw a turtle sunning himself on a log. He walked over and kicked the turtle clear across the river. An alligator lying there asked, "Why did you do that? That turtle wasn't bothering you." "He didn't today," said the elephant, "but twenty years ago I came here for a drink, and he bit me on the trunk. I remember such things because I have turtle recall."

A Hearing Test

An Irish scientist was working with a frog. He cut off it's front left leg, told it to jump, and it jumped. He cut off it's front right leg, told it to jump, and it jumped. He cut off it's back left leg, told it to jump, and it jumped. He cut off it's back right leg told it to jump, and it didn't jump. His conclusion: After cutting off all the frog's legs, the frog loses it's hearing!

Blessed Are The Red-Necked

"What's wrong, Bubba?" asked the pastor. "I need you to pray for my hearing," said Bubba.
The pastor put his hands on Bubba's ears and prayed. When he was done, he asked, "So how's your hearing?" "I don't know," said Bubba. "It isn't until next Tuesday."

Las Vegas Style

There are more Catholic churches than casinos in Las Vegas. Not surprisingly, some worshipers at Sunday services will give casino chips rather than cash when the basket is passed. Since they get chips from many different casinos, the churches send all their collected chips to a nearby Franciscan monastery for sorting. Then the chips are taken to the casinos of origin and cashed in. This is done by the chip monks.

Young Saleswoman

A husband and wife were resting on a beach when they noticed a girl with a travel bag. She approach people with boom boxes and other electronic devices and spoke to them. Occasionally she would hand them something and they would giver her some money, and she would walk off.
"She's probably selling drugs," said the woman.
The man decided to see for himself. The wife watched as her husband walked across the beach to the girl with the travel bag. They spoke briefly, and then her husband returned. "Is she selling drugs," asked the Wife anxiously? "No, she's not," replied her Husband. "She's selling batteries." You don't mean . . . ? "Yup," finished her husband, "she sells c-cells by the sea shore!"

Yacht Club

An Indian in Oklahoma had made it big in the oil leasing business and applied to the Yacht Club in Oklahoma City for membership. When he was refused, he was infuriated. "Why are you so upset?" asked a friend." "This means more to me than just a club membership. I have lived for the day when I could see my Red Son in the Sails Set."

Star of Euphrates

King Ozymandias of Assyria was running low on cash after years of war with the Hittites. His last great possession was the Star of the Euphrates, the most valuable diamond in the ancient world. Desperate, he went to Croesus, the pawnpoker, to ask for a loan. Croesus said, "I'll give you 100,000 dinars for it." "But I paid a million dinars for it," the king protested. "Don't you know who I am? I am the king!" Croesus replied, "When you wish to pawn a star, makes no difference who you are."

Bowling League

Evidence has been found that William Tell and his family were avid bowlers. Unfortunately, all the Swiss league records were destroyed in a fire, so we'll never know for whom the Tells bowled.

Shrinking Patient

A man rushed into a busy doctor's office and shouted, "Doctor! I think I'm shrinking!" The doctor calmly responded, "Now, settle down. You'll just have to be a little patient."

Let Sleeping Lions Lie

A marine biologist developed a race of genetically engineered dolphins that could live forever if they were fed a steady diet of young seagulls. One day, his supply of the birds ran out so he had to go out and trap more. On the way back, he spied two lions asleep on the road. Afraid to wake them, he gingerly stepped over them. Immediately, he was arrested and charged with transporting young gulls across sedate lions for immortal porpoises.

Tate's Watch Company

Back in the 1800s, the Tate's Watch Company of Massachusetts wanted to produce other products, and since they already made the cases for watches, they used them to produce compasses. However, the new compasses were so bad that people often ended up in Canada or Mexico rather than California. This, of course, is the origin of the expression, "He who has a Tate's is lost!"

Even Police Have Their Problems

A thief broke into the local police station and stole all the toilets and urinals, leaving no clues. A spokesperson was quoted as saying, "We have absolutely nothing to go on."

The Power of a Song

An Indian chief was feeling very sick, so he summoned the medicine man. After a brief examination, the medicine man took out a long, thin strip of elk rawhide and gave it to the chief, telling him to bite off, chew, and swallow one inch of the leather every day. After a month, the medicine man returned to see how the chief was feeling. The chief shrugged and said, "The thong is ended, but the malady lingers on."

Viking Census

A famous Viking explorer returned home from a voyage and found his name missing from the town register. His wife insisted on complaining to the local civic official who apologized profusely saying, "I must have taken Leif off my census."

The Power of Plants

A skeptical anthropologist was cataloging South American folk remedies with the assistance of a tribal pujo who indicated that the leaves of a particular fern were a sure cure for any case of constipation. When the anthropologist expressed his doubts, the pujo looked him in the eye and said, "Let me tell you, with fronds like these, you don't need enemas."

The Importance of a Comma

A panda walked into a restaurant and ordered a sandwich. After he had eaten and received his check, he pulled out a gun, fired it several times, then walked out the door. A stunned patron asked the waiter, "What was that all about?" The waiter responded, "That's just the way pandas are," and walked away. The patron didn't know what a panda was, so at home that night he looked up *Panda*, in the dictionary and what he found explained everything: *Panda: A large black-and-white bear-like mammal, native to China; eats shoots and leaves.*

Dough Boy

Many years ago, a baker's assistant called Richard the Pourer, whose job it was to pour the dough mixture in the making of sausage rolls, noted that he was running low on one of the necessary spices. He sent his apprentice to the store to buy more. Unfortunately, upon arriving at the shop, the young man realized that he had forgotten the name of the ingredient. Hoping that the storekeeper might be able to figure it out, he described it to him saying, "It's for Richard the Pourer, for batter for wurst."

Liver Worst

A woman was standing in the butcher shop watching the butcher wait on a Swami. He ordered a pound of liver, and the woman noticed that as the butcher weighed the meat, he kept his thumb on the scales as well. When the Swami left, the woman said to the butcher: "That was a terrible thing you did. I saw you with your thumb on the scales." The butcher said, "Yeah, I should not have done it, but I hate that guy. All he ever does is come in here and order a pound of liver. So every chance I get, I weigh down upon the Swami's liver.

Bird Brain

A young boy was at the beach and he decided to get rid of all the sea gulls. He picked up a bunch of rocks and started throwing them at the gulls. He didn't hit many, but they flew away for a while. Each time they came back, he would throw another rock. In his quest to rid the beach of gulls, he left no tern unstoned.

Snail

A snail walked into a Mercedes-Benz dealership and said he wanted was tired of moving so slowly that he wanted to buy the top of the line model. However, he had one request: he wanted the salesperson to paint a big red *S* on the driver's door. The salesperson replied, "Sir, this is a very expensive and beautiful car. I can't jut paint a red S on the door. The snail turned and headed for the door. The sales person began to calculate what the commission would be and decided that monetary needs trumped aesthetics. The salesperson stopped the snail who was about half-way to the door. "All right, I'll do it, but you must tell me why." "It's really very simple," replied the snail. "When I drive down the street I want people to point at me and exclaim, "Wow! Look at that *S* car go!"

Made in the USA
Lexington, KY
19 December 2019